Amazing Butterflies & Moths

WRITTEN BY
JOHN STILL

PHOTOGRAPHED BY
JERRY YOUNG

Dorling Kindersley · London

A Dorling Kindersley Book

Project editors Scott Steedman and Louise Pritchard
Art editor Ann Cannings
Senior art editor Jacquie Gulliver
Production Louise Barratt

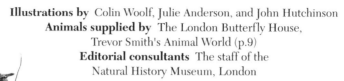

Illustrations by Colin Woolf, Julie Anderson, and John Hutchinson
Animals supplied by The London Butterfly House,
Trevor Smith's Animal World (p.9)
Editorial consultants The staff of the
Natural History Museum, London

First published in Great Britain in 1991 by
Dorling Kindersley Limited
9 Henrietta Street, London WC2E 8PS

A CIP catalogue record for this book is available from the British Library

ISBN 0-86318-549-5

Colour reproduction by Colourscan, Singapore
Typeset by Windsorgraphics, Ringwood, Hampshire
Printed in Italy by A. Mondadori Editore, Verona

Contents

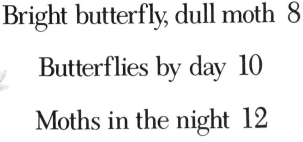

Bright butterfly, dull moth

When people think of butterflies, they see beautiful wings fluttering in the sunlight. When they think of moths, they imagine a dull creature of the night bumping against a light bulb. Some of the time, they are right.

Antenna

Eye

Proboscis

Leg

Front wing

Back wing

What makes a butterfly?
Like all insects, butterflies and moths have six legs, a head, and a body in two parts. They also have two pairs of wings, big eyes, antennae, and a tongue called a proboscis (*pro-boss-kiss*).

Feelers
You can usually tell a moth from a butterfly by its "feelers" or antennae. Most butterflies have little knobs on the end of their antennae. Moths never do, and many have thick antennae that look like feathers.

Butterfly

Moth

False eyes
This moth has false "eyes" on its wings to scare birds.

8

Brilliant blue
This emperor butterfly lives in the steamy jungles of South and Central America.

Wings up
When they rest, most butterflies close their wings up over their backs. Moths, meanwhile, usually sit with their wings flat.

Common windmill butterfly

Chrysalis starting to open

Magic changes
Every butterfly and moth starts life as an egg. A tiny caterpillar hatches from the egg. Later the caterpillar throws off its skin to reveal a hard case (called the chrysalis or pupa). Then, as if by magic, the case splits open and out crawls a grown-up butterfly or moth.

Bright moths
There are many more moths than butterflies – about 150,000 kinds altogether. Not all are grey or brown. Fashionable ladies even wore the glittering wings of some moths as jewellery.

Dull butterflies
There are about 20,000 different kinds of butterfly in the world. Some of them aren't much to look at.

Butterfly just hatched from chrysalis

Butterflies by day

Because of their brilliant colours, butterflies are one of the most loved groups of animals in the world. Many people plant flowers in their gardens to attract them.

Life in the sun
Butterflies need sunlight to warm their bodies. So next time you see one basking in the sunshine, remember that it isn't just being lazy.

Too drunk to fly
Some butterflies drink the juices of rotten fruit. If the fruit has turned to cider, the butterflies can get so drunk they can't fly!

Fighting butterflies?

Some butterflies fight with one another over a piece of land or even a patch of sunshine. Luckily, they're not tough enough to really hurt each other.

Watering holes
In hot countries, big groups of butterflies can be seen on damp ground, drinking water.

Dainty eaters
Butterflies use their proboscis to suck up liquid foods – usually nectar from flowers. The proboscis works rather like a straw.

And so to bed...
Most butterflies look for a quiet spot to spend the night. This is usually a leaf or the tip of a grass stalk where birds won't find them. They will often return to the same spot every night.

Antennae for "smelling" and for "feeling"

Two faces
Like many butterflies, the lacewing looks quite different with its wings open.

Lacy wings
This butterfly's wings look like lace curtains – which is why it's called the lacewing.

Moths in the night

Many moths are attracted to bright lights. For years, no one knew why. Now we believe it is probably because they find their way in the dark by using the moon and stars to guide them.

Invisible moths
Moths that fly at night have to be dark or well-disguised, so that they can hide away during the day.

Reaching the bottom
Like butterflies, many moths feed on nectar. Some have an extremely long proboscis for reaching the bottom of deep flowers. One African moth has a proboscis three times as long as its body!

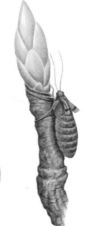

Wingless
The winter moth lives its whole, short life in the dead of winter. Female moths have no wings at all, but crawl about like bugs with winter coats on.

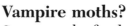

Vampire moths?
Some moths feed on nothing but the eye liquids of cattle, deer, or even elephants. The Asian vampire moth can even pierce an animal's skin and drink its blood!

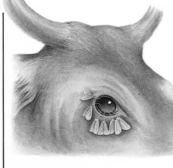

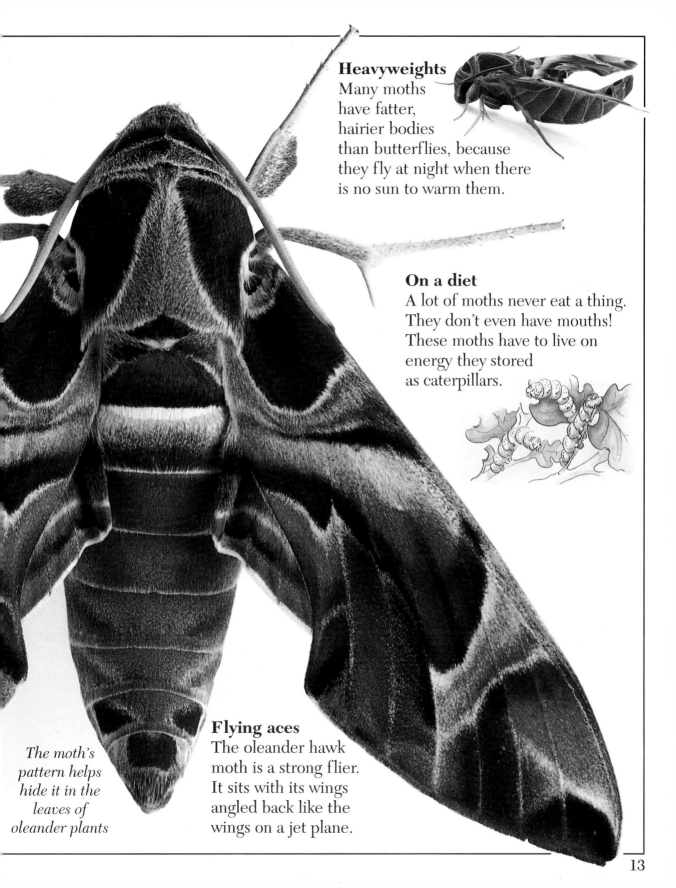

Heavyweights
Many moths
have fatter,
hairier bodies
than butterflies, because
they fly at night when there
is no sun to warm them.

On a diet
A lot of moths never eat a thing.
They don't even have mouths!
These moths have to live on
energy they stored
as caterpillars.

*The moth's
pattern helps
hide it in the
leaves of
oleander plants*

Flying aces
The oleander hawk
moth is a strong flier.
It sits with its wings
angled back like the
wings on a jet plane.

Colours of the rainbow

Butterflies come in every colour you can imagine – and some you can't.

The peacock
This European butterfly is dull brown on the underside. When it flashes its wings open, the bright colours are a startling sight.

Gathering sunbeams
Many butterflies have a lot of black on their wings. The dark scales soak up sunlight, to warm the butterfly up.

See-through wings
Some butterflies have hardly any scales on their wings. They can be very hard to see.

Sweet dreams
All over the world, people believe that butterflies are human souls. The Finnish people say that when you dream, your butterfly soul flutters peacefully above your bed.

The knobs on the ends of its antennae identify the peacock as a butterfly not a moth

Tiled wings
The wing of a butterfly is covered in thousands of tiny scales of different colours. The scales overlap like tiles on a roof to create the pattern you see.

On the fringe
At the edge of its wings, a butterfly's scales are long and stringy. Close up, they look like the fringe on a tablecloth.

Seeing the invisible
Butterflies and moths can see ultra-violet light which is invisible to us. Photographs taken on special film show that many flowers and butterflies are decorated with ultra-violet designs.

Senses

Butterflies and moths can see, smell, and taste. But they don't use these senses in the same way you do.

Small sense organs for receiving smell are scattered over the surface of the antennae

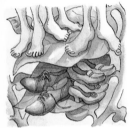

Sensitive feet
You taste with your tongue. But many butterflies and moths taste leaves with their feet!

Smelly radar
Female moths attract males by letting off a special perfume. Males "smell" the perfume with their antennae, which can 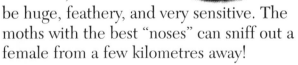 be huge, feathery, and very sensitive. The moths with the best "noses" can sniff out a female from a few kilometres away!

Don't you smell nice
A male butterfly may have a yellow brush on his rear end. He dips this in a special perfume and dusts it over a female, to get her in the mood for romance.

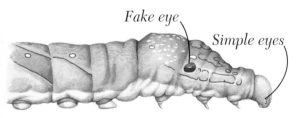

Fake eye

Simple eyes

Nearly blind
Most caterpillars have twelve eyes. But each one can see no more than light or dark. A few kinds have no eyes at all.

Silent night
Butterflies and moths don't have ears like we do. But some moths have a kind of "ear" on the side of their bodies. They need it to listen out for bats, which track them down in the dark using high-pitched squeaks.

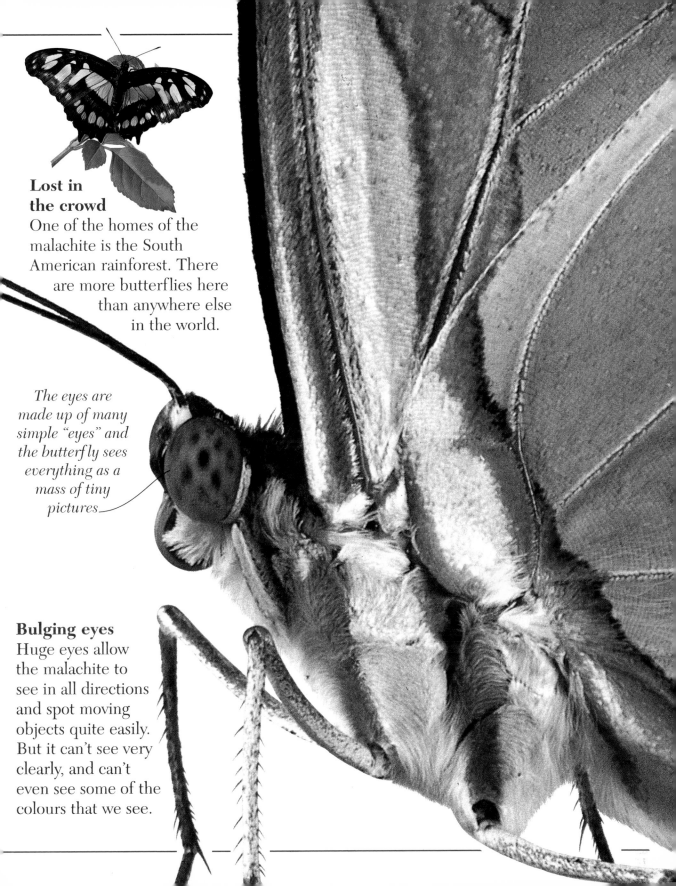

Lost in the crowd
One of the homes of the malachite is the South American rainforest. There are more butterflies here than anywhere else in the world.

The eyes are made up of many simple "eyes" and the butterfly sees everything as a mass of tiny pictures

Bulging eyes
Huge eyes allow the malachite to see in all directions and spot moving objects quite easily. But it can't see very clearly, and can't even see some of the colours that we see.

Amazing shapes and sizes

The biggest moths and butterflies are the size of birds. With its wings open, a giant atlas moth may measure 30 cm across – that's as big as a magpie! Even its caterpillar is twice as long as your middle finger.

Snake eyes
The atlas moth is found from the Himalayas to Bali. The tip of its wing is patterned to look like a snake's head.

Comet moth or Madagascan moon moth

Now here's a tail!
Many butterflies and moths have tails on their wings to disguise their shape. The comet moth from Madagascar has the most impressive tail of all.

The invisible butterfly

Some butterflies have wings like church windows. The glasswing butterfly lives deep in the jungle, where it flies close to the ground and is very hard to see.

Plume moth

You could almost do the dusting with a white plume moth. It has four wings, like all moths, but they branch out to look like feathers.

Little and large...

The Queen Alexandra butterfly from New Guinea can be 28 cm across. That's the size of a blackbird. The smallest butterfly, the South American pygmy blue, is only 1 cm across – no wider than your thumbnail!

To be or not to bee

This unusual moth from Sri Lanka has see-through wings, too. It looks just like a bee, and even flies in the daytime like a bee.

...and teeny weeny!

Some leaf miner moths are even smaller – just 3 mm from wing tip to wing tip. That's not as wide as the lead of a pencil! The caterpillars are so tiny that they live *inside* leaves.

Is it . . .

Butterflies and moths spend a lot of time hiding from their enemies. Many of them are masters of disguise.

...a monster?
Most of the time the puss moth caterpillar is green and hard to notice. But bother it and it will flash its gruesome "face" and whip its tail around. It isn't bluffing, either. It can spit acid if it has to!

...going to sting me?
This harmless European moth keeps its enemies away by looking exactly like a nasty hornet.

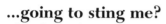

...a rolled leaf?
Even the chrysalis has to keep out of trouble. This owl butterfly chrysalis blends in by copying a dead leaf.

...a nasty mess?
Sometimes it's a good idea to look completely unappetising. The chrysalis of the black hairstreak butterfly sits on a leaf, looking like a bird dropping.

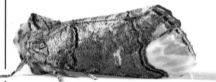

...a broken twig?
The buff-tip moth sits on a branch pretending to be a boring twig. The light marks on its wing tips look like the raw end where the twig has been broken off.

...nothing at all?
Many moths or butterflies have confusing patterns to disguise the shape of their wings and fool their attackers.

...a dead twig?
It looks like a useless little twig. What it *doesn't* look like is the chrysalis of a beautiful brown and cream butterfly.

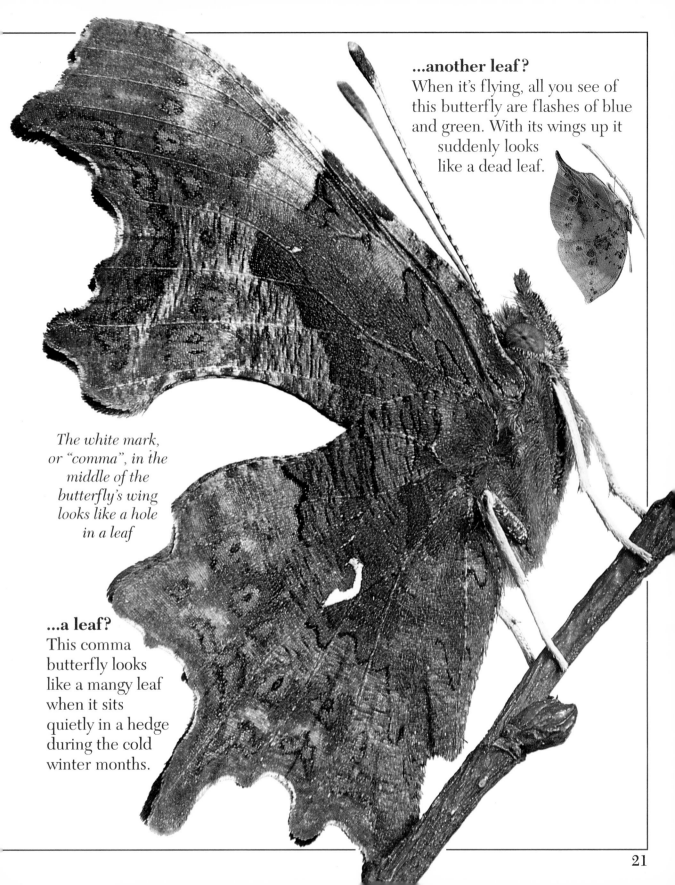

...another leaf?

When it's flying, all you see of this butterfly are flashes of blue and green. With its wings up it suddenly looks like a dead leaf.

The white mark, or "comma", in the middle of the butterfly's wing looks like a hole in a leaf

...a leaf?

This comma butterfly looks like a mangy leaf when it sits quietly in a hedge during the cold winter months.

Poisonous butterflies

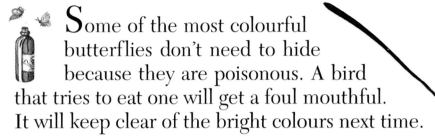

Some of the most colourful butterflies don't need to hide because they are poisonous. A bird that tries to eat one will get a foul mouthful. It will keep clear of the bright colours next time.

Hidden spines
Some caterpillars can give you a nasty rash if you brush against them. The flannel moth caterpillar has stinging spines buried in its hair.

Not so jolly Roger
The death's head hawk moth has a weird skull and crossbones pattern on its back. Not surprisingly, people think it's bad luck if one of them flies into their house at night.

Poisons
The poison in a butterfly's body comes from the plants it ate as a caterpillar. The monarch caterpillar feeds on the deadly milkweed plant.

A small postman's colours advertise its awful taste!

Postman butterfly
The small postman is found from Mexico to Chile. The caterpillars feed on poisonous passionflower vines.

Harmless   *Poisonous*

No it isn't...yes it is!
The butterfly on the left has the same colours and patterns as the poisonous plain tiger on the right. Birds leave it alone, too, but it isn't really poisonous!

Two of a kind
Some kinds of butterfly copy each other's colours. This one looks just like the small postman, and this time it is just as poisonous.

Smelly zebras
Zebra butterflies don't just taste bad, they even smell bad. The nasty pong warns their enemies to leave them in peace. At night, zebras snooze together in big, extra-smelly groups.

23

Wings that wink

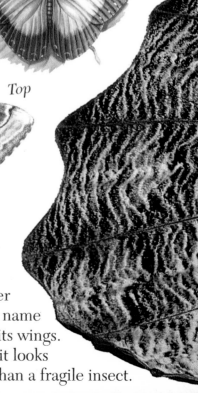

Many butterflies and moths have marks on their wings which look like eyes. A quick flash of these "eyespots" startles their enemies, so they can make a quick getaway.

Flying after butter

People used to think that butterflies were fairies in disguise. The name butterfly may come from the strange belief that these sneaky fairies stole butter and milk!

Too many eyes

Fake eyes may fool birds into attacking the wrong end of the butterfly. The pearly eye has a row of eyes along the outer edge of its wings, to keep hungry birds away from its real head.

Blink and flash

Morpho butterflies have eyespots on the bottom of their wings and brilliant colours on the top. If a bird isn't fooled by the eyes, it may well be dazzled by the flashing colours.

Bottom

Top

Blinking eyes

Sometimes false eyes are hidden away on the bottom wing. When the moth or butterfly is threatened, it spreads its wings and flashes its "eyes"

Sneaky snakes

Caterpillars may use eyespots to fool birds into thinking they are small snakes.

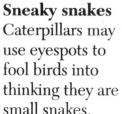

Owl butterfly

The owl butterfly is bigger than a sparrow. It gets its name from the huge "eyes" on its wings. Perched on a tree trunk, it looks more like a hungry bird than a fragile insect.

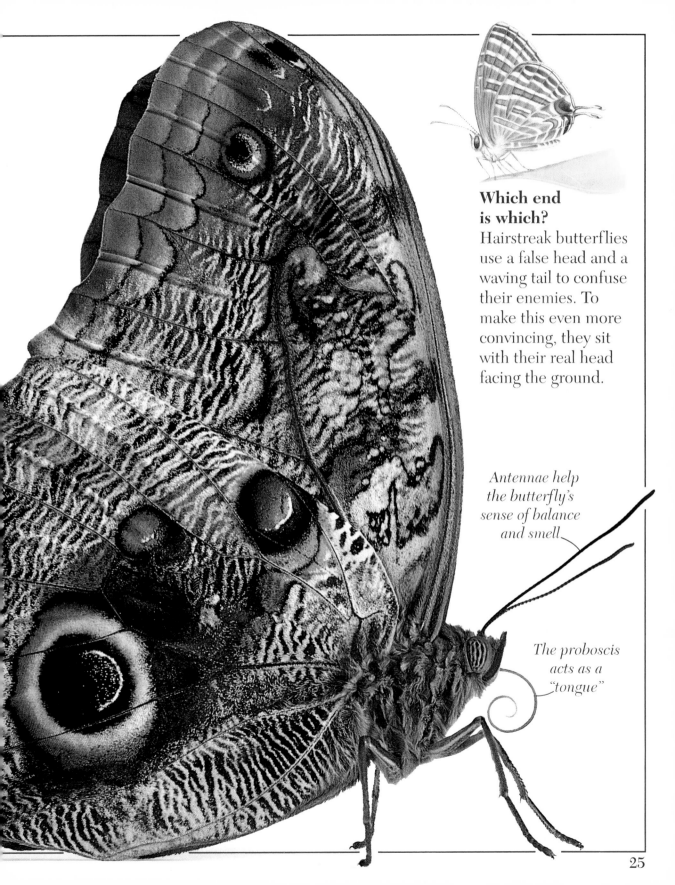

Which end is which?
Hairstreak butterflies use a false head and a waving tail to confuse their enemies. To make this even more convincing, they sit with their real head facing the ground.

Antennae help the butterfly's sense of balance and smell

The proboscis acts as a "tongue"

Getting away from it all

Many butterflies and moths are great travellers. They may travel long distances to escape the hot weather, or even to find a new home if theirs becomes too crowded.

New pastures
Butterflies often travel in search of new spots to live and lay their eggs. The red admiral flies from Africa across the Mediterranean Sea to Europe to do this.

Fluttering by
Butterflies have good control over their flight movements and can make sudden landings. Morphos can fly well enough to out-manoeuvre most birds in the air.

The big sleep
Butterflies and moths that live in cold places sleep through the winter. Some of them survive the winter as eggs, caterpillars, or pupae. The adults of other species bed down in a cave, under a leaf, or even in a house.

Clouds of butterflies

One of the biggest clouds of butterflies ever seen measured 400 km across. More than a million butterflies passed overhead, *every minute*, for a whole day!

Out of the sun

The bogong moth likes to escape the hot Australian summer. It flies long distances to find a cool mountain cave to snooze in.

The monarch butterfly can fly 130 km per day

The monarch

In the autumn, this butterfly flies from Canada to the warm parts of America and Mexico. In spring, some fly all the way back to Canada.

Roosting

When the monarch butterflies arrive at their winter quarters in Mexico, they gather in a huge mass. Thousands of butterflies may occupy one tree.

From egg to butterfly

Butterflies and moths change three times to become adults. They change from egg to caterpillar to chrysalis to adult. This amazing change is called metamorphosis (*met-a-mor-foh-sis*).

1 The zebra butterfly lays her eggs singly on the tips of leaves. A tiny caterpillar will hatch from each egg and start to eat straight away.

Long-lived butterfly
The adult zebra butterfly can live for as long as eight months – a long life for a butterfly.

Two weeks old

One day old

2 The caterpillar begins to put on weight. It has to shed its skin four or five times to allow it to grow bigger. Then it is time for it to find a suitable spot to turn into a chrysalis.

One week old

3 The chrysalis hangs from a silken pad attached to a plant. It is cleverly disguised to help it hide amongst the leaves. Inside, the caterpillar's body reforms into a butterfly.

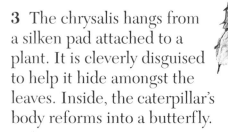

4 The adult butterfly crawls out of the chrysalis. It must wait for its wings to dry and expand before it can fly.

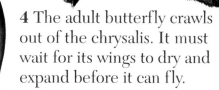

Farm moths

Moth caterpillars often spin silk to protect them while they pupate. Silk used to make some clothes comes from silkmoth farms!

Beware!

The slug caterpillar is brightly coloured to warn predators that its spines sting like nettles.

Just a drop

The shiny pupa of the tree nymph hangs among leaves. It reflects the light and looks like a drop of water.

The bold stripes of a zebra butterfly warn off enemies

Pure gold

Chrysalis means "gold". The name was given as many chrysalises have gold spots on them to disguise them.